# 表里山河 黄河

YELLOW RIVER

MOUNTAINS AND RIVERS OF SHANXI

贾新田 主编



山西出版传媒集团 山西教育出版社

《表里山河》


主　编　贾新田

学术统筹　王修筑

图片统筹　武　涛

内文撰稿　王宝库　刘晓露

英文翻译　王介功　崔　璟

设计总监　王春声

篆　刻　唐　晋

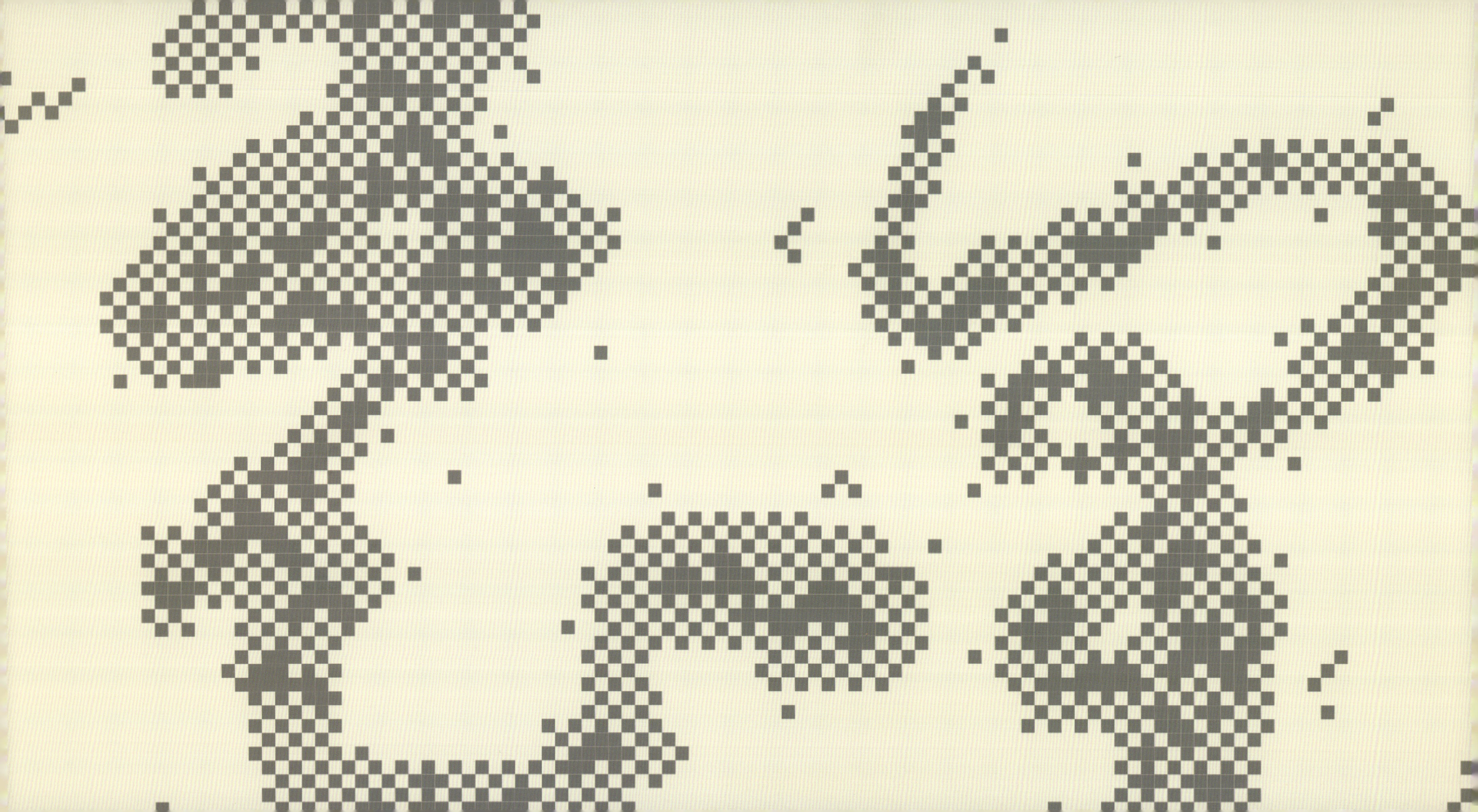

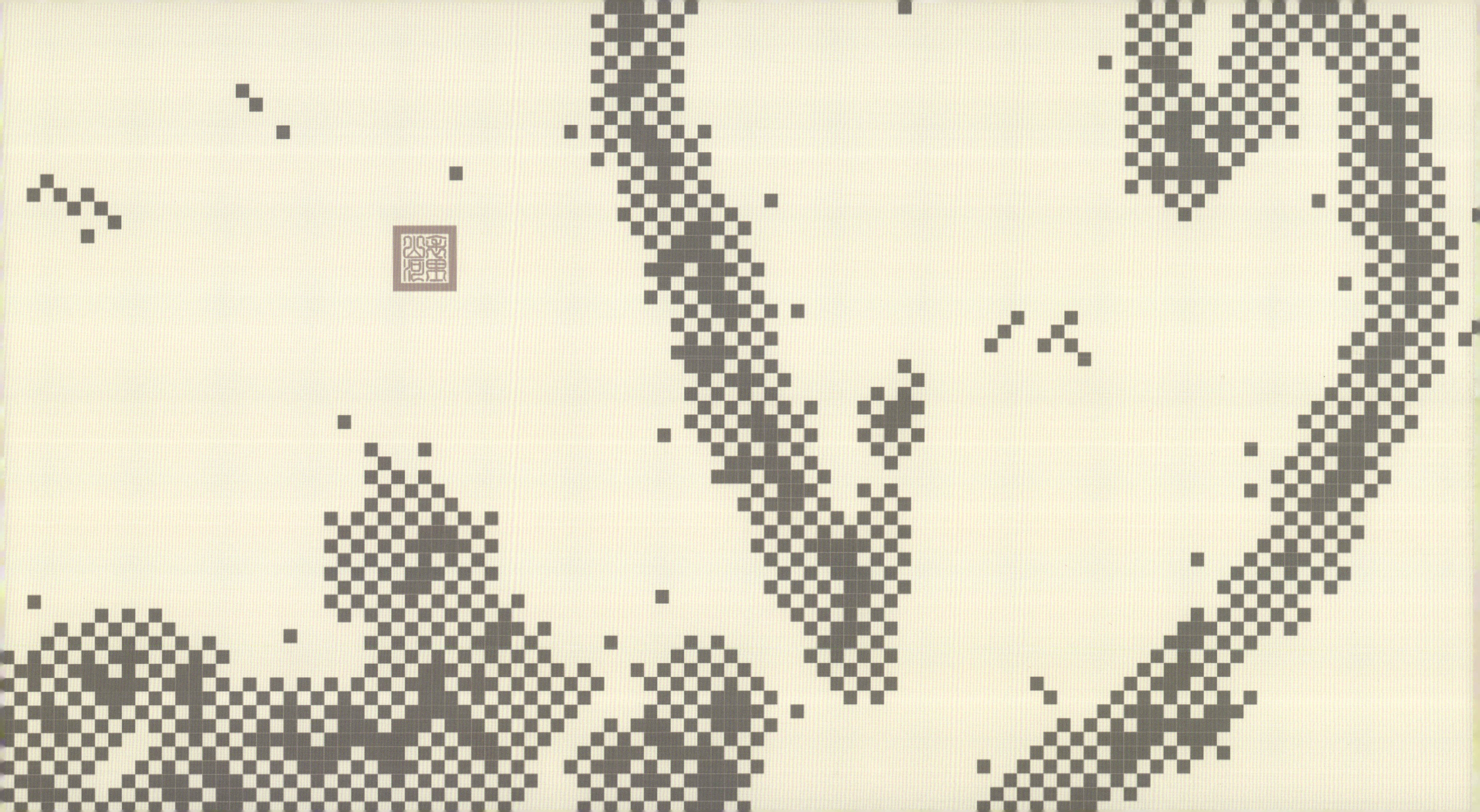

汾澮縈流於右漳沁包絡於左則原隰可以灌注漕粟可以轉輸矣且夫越臨晉泝龍門則涇渭之間可折箠而下也出天井下壺關邯鄲井陘而東不可以惟吾所向乎是故天下之形勢必有取於山西也

山西之形勢最爲完固
關中而外吾必首及夫
山西蓋語其東則太行
爲之屏障其西則大河
爲之襟帶於北則大漠
陰山爲之外蔽而勾注
雁門爲之內險於南則
首陽底柱析城王屋諸
山濱河而錯峙又南則
孟津潼關皆吾門戶也

摄影：尚建周

乾坤湾

On the west of the Taihang Mountains on the second-level platform of the mainland of China, there is a province named "Shanxi" (literally means "on the west of the Mountains"). The origin of its name comes from its location.

Shanxi is the present name, and it was called "Hedong" (literally means "on the east of the River") in ancient times, which was derived from its location on the east of the Yellow River.

The Mountains and the River from which the ancient and modern names of Shanxi originated are extraordinary. The Taihang Mountains are the backbone of the Chinese nation, the pillar of the Chinese territory. The Yellow River is the mother river of the Chinese nation and the emblem, flag and totem of Chinese culture.

The name of Shanxi changes with the change of the capital. In the heyday of the Yellow River civilization, the capital was Chang'an, and the Yellow River was its eastern barrier. Therefore, the province on the east of the Yellow River was named "Hedong". In the booming period of marine civilization, the capital is Beijing, and the Taihang Mountains are its western barrier. So, the province is named "Shanxi" for the similar reason. Being an auxiliary to the ancient and modern capitals of China, Shanxi is very important. Because of this, Shanxi has long history, rich culture and infinite charm.

When we say "knowing Shanxi from the mountains and rivers", we mean to learn the history, culture and charm of Shanxi through the outer and inner parts of Shanxi.

The outer part here refers to the Taihang Mountains, the Yellow River and the Great Wall on the periphery of Shanxi, while the inner part refers to the rivers, mountains and cultural relics of Shanxi. Gu Zuyu, a geographer in the early Qing Dynasty, gave a wonderful statement on this:

Judging from the physical features, Shanxi is closed and complete. I would like to consider Shanxi first beyond the central part of China. To the east, the Taihang Mountains act as a barrier; to the west, the big river is the belt; to the north, the desert and the Yin Mountains are the outer cover, while the Gouzhu Mountain and the Yanmen Pass are the inner barrier; to the south, the Shouyang Mountain, Dizhu Mountain, Xicheng Mountain and Wangwu Mountain scatter along the rivers; to the south of these mountains, Mengjin County and Tong Pass are its gateway. With the Fen River and Hui River on the right, and the Zhang River and Qin River on the left, the fields can be watered and grains transported. And if you go across Linjin Town and continue upstream over Longmen Port, you can easily go down along the Jing River and Wei River. When you go out of the basin here and down Huguan County, along Handan City and Jingxing County to the east, you can reach everywhere. Therefore, considering the physical features of China, Shanxi is the irreplaceable communications center.

This passage outlines the mountains, rivers, passes and ports in Shanxi, and provides a geographical map of ancient Shanxi.

The division of Shanxi's cultural and tourism resources is diverse, but there are always overlaps and omissions. The division based on the three major sectors of the Taihang Mountains, the Yellow River, and the Great Wall is not only scientific and accurate, but also well-documented in history.

It is scientific and accurate. The area of Shanxi is an irregular parallelogram. The Fen River, the mother river of the people of Shanxi, passes through the land from the north to the south. The Taihang Mountains Sector is to the east, and the Yellow River Valley and the Lüliang Mountains are to the west. To the north of the source of Fen River is the so-called the Great Wall Sector.

It is well-documented in history. As Gu Zuyu said, "On the east, the Taihang Mountains act as a barrier." This refers to the Taihang Mountains Sector. "To the west, the big river is the belt" refers to the Yellow River Sector. "To the north, the desert and the Yin Mountains are the outer cover, while the Gouzhu Mountain and the Yanmen Pass are the inner barrier" refers to the Great Wall Sector. As for the central and southern regions, they belong to the Taihang Mountains Sector and the Yellow River Sector with a clear boundary.

In terms of time, the Taihang Mountains, the Yellow River and the Great Wall have long histories, and there are no other comparable geographical things in China. In terms of space, the geographical advantages occupied by these three sectors are even higher. In terms of culture, the richness and uniqueness of the culture here are worth deep exploration. If you sink into it and concentrate on it, you will definitely harvest a lot.

中国大陆第二级台地上的太行山西侧，有一个以“山西”为名号的省份。其名称之缘起，即因位于太行山西侧而得之。

山西是今名，其古称曰“河东”，因位于黄河之东而得之。

山西古今名称缘起的这一山一河，非比寻常。太行山是中华民族的脊骨、中华大厦的栋梁。黄河则是中华民族的母亲河和中华文化的徽号、旗帜与图腾。

山西古今名称之演变，系因国都的改变而改变。黄河文明鼎盛期的最佳国都在长安，黄河乃其东部屏障，斯省所在之地域因而称名“河东”；海洋文明勃兴期的国都定位北京，太行山乃其西部屏障，故斯地名之曰“山西”。山西其地是中国都城的左辅或右弼，因而地理位置得天独厚，十分重要。正因为如此，斯地因而富含了绵远悠长的历史、丰硕厚重的文化和魅力无穷的风韵。

我们说“表里山河看山西”，就是说要透过山西的“表”和“里”看山西的历史、看山西的文化、看山西的风韵。

此处所谓“表”者，是形成山西外围的太行山、黄河与塞外长城，“里”则是山西其地的河流山川与文物风情。清代著名学者顾祖禹对此有十分精彩的表述：

山西之形势，最为完固。关中而外，吾必首及夫山西。盖语其东，则太行为之屏障；其西，则大河为之襟带；于北，则大漠、阴山为之外蔽，而勾注、雁门为之内险；于南，则首阳、底柱、析城、王屋诸山，滨河而错峙；又南，则孟津、潼关，皆吾门户也。汾、浍萦流于右，漳、沁包络于左，则原隰可以灌注，漕粟可以转输矣！且夫越临晋，溯龙门，则泾、渭之间，可折箠而下也。出天井，下壶关，邯郸、井陉而东，不可以惟吾所向乎？是故天下之形势，必有取于山西也！

这一段话概括地勾勒出一幅山西全境雄关险隘、襟山带河的水陆形胜图，令人发思古之幽情，平添感慨。

山西文化和旅游资源之板块划分，方法非止一端，但总会产生重叠或遗漏而有失偏颇。作太行、黄河、长城之三大板块划分，既科学精准，又于史有据，可谓是“表里山河看山西”之全息彰显也。

我们说如此划分科学精准，是因为山西地域呈不规则的平行四边形，山西人民的母亲河——汾河由北而南自山西大地穿过，东则太行山板块，西乃黄河流域及其所依傍之吕梁山系。汾源以北的另一方地域，就是所谓长城板块。

我们说如此划分于史有据，即顾祖禹所云“其东，则太行为之屏障”，太行山板块也；“其西，则大河为之襟带”，黄河板块也；“于北，则大漠、阴山为之外蔽，而勾注、雁门为之内险”，长城板块也。至于中南部地域则分属太行、黄河两大板块，界限分明，不会重叠。

就时间而言之，太行、黄河、长城的历史之悠久，在大中国的同类地理事物中无有可与攀比者；就空间而言之，此三大板块所占据的地理区位优势更是高踞首位；就文化和韵味而言之，此三大板块文化蕴涵的厚重与丰硕，以及韵味的奇奥与独特，既一言难尽其详，又因观者的不同而各有品味。倘能沉身于其中并且潜心于其内，必定感触良多而收获宏丰。

# YELLOW RIVER 黄河

# 黄河

YELLOW RIVER

黄河是中国第二长河，发源于青海省青藏高原，自西向东分别流经青海、四川、甘肃、宁夏、内蒙古、陕西、山西、河南及山东 9 个省（自治区），最后流入渤海，呈“几”字形，故有“几字黄河”之称。

# 黄河礼赞

TRIBUTE TO THE YELLOW RIVER

黄河发源于巴颜喀拉山，涓涓清流渐渐形成澎湃之势，向东方流淌，过青、川、甘、宁、蒙，纳百川千河，声势渐大，龙吟虎啸，在晋蒙交界处的老牛湾折而向南，于秦晋大峡谷中历经万家寨的湍激、大同碛的起伏、壶口的跌宕、龙门的喧嚣，清流因着厚土的沉淀变为浑黄，在垣曲出山西境，复向东流，越豫至鲁，汇入渤海。它，就是中华民族的母亲河——黄河。

百转千回的黄河奔流到吉县龙王辿之后，河床骤然变窄，狭如壶口。滔滔黄河水自壶口跌入巨穴深潭之内，但见白浪翻滚，水花飞溅，云雾腾空，谷涧起雷，水底有龙掀巨浪，岸旁现雨挂长虹，远处可闻其声，望之似巨壶沸腾，此即闻名遐迩的“壶口飞瀑”，乃世界第一黄色大瀑布，亦是万里黄河的精华所在，是具有典型性和代表性的景观与标识。

黄河自北向南沿秦晋大峡谷奔腾而来，至吕梁山脉南端，两岸峭崖对峙，壁立千仞，形如门阙。汹涌不羁的黄河水在门阙内横冲直撞，雷霆万钧，怒吼着跌入谷底，涌出龙门。如此奇观，古人称之曰“禹门三级浪，平地一声雷”。相传每至农历春三月，鲤鱼逆水而上，游至此处，跃入其门者可化为龙，故称“龙门”。

相传，大禹当年治理水患时导河积石，疏浚吕梁山，开凿龙门口，遂令黄河至此夺峡而出，一泻千里。后人为了纪念大禹治水之功，因而尊龙门为“禹门”。

万里黄河大曲者有九而小湾倍之，号称“天下黄河九曲十八弯”。九曲十八弯的黄河在秦晋大峡谷内令人惊奇地酿造了弯度几乎成圆圈的石楼湾与太极图般的永和乾坤湾，继之又有风陵渡、大禹渡、茅津渡，以至三门峡，不但风景秀丽，而且历史悠久、文化厚重，令人睹景生情，一步三叹。

黄河不但是中华民族的母亲河，亦系中华文明肇始的源头和起点，更是中华文化的徽号、图腾与旌幡。

黄河水百折千转，屈曲回圜，跌宕起伏，汹涌澎湃，克服千难万险，一往无前，汇入大海，象征中华民族在历史长河中饱经沧桑而绝不气馁的精神和认定目标便勇往直前的气魄。日寇入侵、民族危亡、国难当头时，那首著名的抗日救亡歌曲，便是《黄河大合唱》。

黄河岸边，矗立着后土祠、秋风楼、鹳鹊楼、莺莺塔；黄河流域，盐池的故事一直在流传。

黄河之水，奔流到海，润我华夏。

The Yellow River originates from Bayan Har Mountains, and surges to the east through the provinces of Qinghai, Sichuan, Gansu, Ningxia and Inner Mongolia. It gathers hundreds of springs and streams, flows furiously with the sound of growing momentum, and turns sharply to the south at the Laoniu Bay at the junction of Shanxi and Inner Mongolia. Flowing through the Qin-Jin Grand Canyon, it rushes in the Wanjiazhai Reservoir, heaves at the Datong Gravel Shoal, falls at the Hukou Waterfall, roars in the Longmen Port, and then flows out of Shanxi from Yuanqu County and turns east again. With loess, the clear river becomes muddy yellow, flows through Henan, and empties into the Bohai Sea in Shandong Province at last. It is the Yellow River, the mother river of the Chinese nation.

After the Yellow River reaches Longwangchan in Jixian County, the riverbed suddenly turns as narrow as the spout of a kettle. The water falls into the deep pool from here, with rolling and foaming waves, splashing spindrifts, rising water mist, thunderclaps, and a rainbow hanging on the river bank, just like in a giant boiling kettle. This is the Hukou Waterfall (literally means the kettle spout waterfall), which is not only the world's largest yellow waterfall, but also the typical and representative landscape of the Yellow River.

The Yellow River rushes from north to south along the Qin-Jin Grand Canyon to the southern end of the Lüliang Mountains, with steep cliff on each side like a giant gate. The roaring Yellow River rampages through the gate down the valley. The ancient people called this wonder as "The sound of surfs in the Gate of Yu is as loud as a thunder". According to legend, during every third month of the lunar year, carp would swim upstream to this place and those who jump into the gate can be transformed into dragons, hence it is called the Dragon Gate or the Longmen Port.

According to legend, in order to control the floods, the Great Yu led people to dredge the Yellow River in the Jishi Mountain and the Lüliang Mountains and cut the Dragon Gate, so that the river came out of the canyon here and plunged thousands of miles. In order to commemorate the achievements of the Great Yu, posterity honoured the Dragon Gate as the Gate of Yu or the Yumen Port.

There are nine big meanders and eighteen small ones in the Yellow River. The most beautiful ones are the U-shaped Shilou Bay and the S-shaped Qiankun Bay, followed by Fengling Port, Dayu Port, Maojin Port, and Sanmenxia Reservoir. The beautiful scenery and the long history here impress visitors a lot.

The Yellow River is not only the mother river of the Chinese nation, but also its birthplace, and is even the symbol, totem and flag of the Chinese culture.

The course of the Yellow River to the sea is a symbol of the Chinese people's indomitable spirit after experiencing tribulations and the courage to push straight forward to the destination. And there was a famous song named *The Yellow River Cantata* during the War of Resistance Against Japanese Aggression when the country was in danger.

On the banks of the Yellow River, there stands Houtu Temple, Qiufeng Tower, Guanque Tower and Yingying Tower. In the Yellow River Basin, the story of the Salt Lake is passing down from generation to generation.

The Yellow River, which rushes restlessly into the sea, nourishes the land of China.

摄影 饶二保

# 黄河，中华民族的母亲河

The Yellow River, the mother river of the Chinese nation

# 偏关 老牛湾

这里是黄河入晋的起点，是黄河劈开晋陕大峡谷一路向南的开端，以黄河和长城在此握手而闻名遐迩。澎湃黄河，迤逦长城，中华民族的两大精神象征，在这个有着朴实名字的地方庄严交汇。今天，她安详的姿态掩不住沧桑的影子，这是历史深处的回声和岁月悠长的馈赠。

摄影 段保生

偏关 老牛湾

摄影 王修筑

偏关 老牛湾

摄影 王兴刚





## 偏关 老牛湾老码头

淤积的沙，那是黄河流淌过的水位痕迹；坚毅的山，那是黄河途经此地的目击者。而停泊的小船边，那是摆渡者还是打鱼人？天地苍茫，万物静默，但这古老的码头并不孤独，因为遗忘从来未曾发生。

万家寨水利枢纽

## 偏关 万家寨黄河水利枢纽

黄河万家寨水利枢纽离老牛湾不远，建于晋蒙峡谷中，是上世纪建造的山西最大的引黄入晋工程项目，以供水、发电为主，兼有防洪、防凌等综合功能，为干旱缺水的山西做出了巨大的贡献。母亲河无私地哺育着三晋大地。

发源于平鲁穿行于偏关的百里关河，是黄河的一级支流。春分之际，河面上还有碎冰随波漂流，在阳光下闪闪发亮。关河蜿蜒行进，至此汇入黄河。关河口村因之得名。村落中，有农户和渔夫，有鸡鸣与犬吠，有一排排石窑洞……令人久久流连的，是塞外的黄土风情，是久违的淳朴民风。

## 偏关 关河口

摄影 王修筑

# 河曲 黄河老桥

上世纪修建的水泥桥曾是黄河上一大奇观。今天的夕阳下，老桥静静伫立，黄河水如同凝固一般。凝固的不仅是黄河水，还有时光。时光不老，依稀往梦似曾见，老桥的故事还在。

河曲 龙口水电站

摄影 武 涛

## 河曲 娘娘滩

位于黄河中的娘娘滩，是一座面积不大的「凸」形小岛。晨曦中，晋、陕、蒙三地的雄鸡不约而同引吭高歌，唤醒了这里沉睡的人和草木。天渐渐亮了，整齐的田舍、茂密的树林，以及四周平缓的黄河水，都明媚起来。岛上人家，俨然便是幸福的桃源中人。

## 临县 碛口

『九曲黄河第一镇』『水旱码头小都会』，都是碛口的美称。碛口是古时山西防御匈奴的要塞，是明清乃至之后很长一段时间晋陕商道的水陆交通枢纽。曾经金戈铁马，曾经熙攘喧嚣；如今铅华洗净，繁华褪去，大河的样貌却一如从前，沉浑而平静。夏日，山巍峨，树葱郁；冬天，白雪无声地覆盖了屋顶。苍茫天地间，河水冰封，陷入沉思之中。

临县 碛口

摄影 武 涛

## 石楼 石楼湾

由北向南一路奔流的大河，至石楼，突然向东拐去，然后，再绕回来。一个华丽大湾赫然呈现。湾内山体状如神龟，湾外黄土巨石巍巍然。黄河盛大而隽永，沉默而笃定，正在积蓄力量，准备继续出发。

摄影 徐劲松

石楼 石楼湾

摄影 武涛

## 石楼 辛关渡口

这个地处大山深处的渡口，因一九三六年二月毛泽东率红军总部在此登陆入晋而被人熟知。那正是决定中国革命前途和命运的关键时刻。现在的辛关渡，已是晋陕水陆码头，人们的生活今非昔比，脸上洋溢着喜悦的笑容。

## 永和 乾坤湾段

黄河奔涌至晋陕峡谷的乾坤湾段，在这里自北而南形成了七道张弛自如的大湾，它们是目前中国干流河道中规模最大的蛇曲群。空中俯瞰，山抱着河，河绕着山，黄河气势磅礴地蜿蜒行进，渐渐消失在遥远的地平线。

摄影：王凌云



## 永和 黄河蛇曲之英雄湾

英雄湾俗称『漩涡湾』，区域中有一处红军崖。为纪念红军东征时的英雄，永和人民称此处为『英雄湾』。在群山的衬托中，英雄精神巍然不倒；在流水的吟唱中，英雄的事迹代代相传。

摄影 武将

永和 黄河蛇曲之白家山湾

摄影 解学红

永和 黄河蛇曲之乾坤湾

摄影/刘素良

# 永和 黄河蛇曲之乾坤湾

# 永和 黄河蛇曲之仙人湾

大宁 马头关黄河公路大桥

## 吉县 壶口瀑布

一路缓缓流淌的大河，到达吉县，已至晋陕峡谷末端，即将成为世界上最大的黄色瀑布。两岸山峰夹峙，河口骤然收紧，落差猛然增大，让黄河以挣脱一切束缚的钢铁意志，怒吼着冲下『壶口』。当巨大的能量得以释放，我们的母亲河，展现出她最激昂、最奋进的一面。此刻的黄河，不屈不挠，勇往直前——这就是英雄热血，这就是民族魂魄。

摄影 黄正东

摄影 王凌云

吉县 壶口瀑布

摄影 武 涛

# 吉县 壶口瀑布

摄影 李安国

吉县 壶口瀑布

摄影 王华

摄影 王凌云





# 吉县 壶口瀑布

摄影 尚建周

摄影 尚建周





# 万荣 后土祠、秋风楼

两千多年前，汉武帝吟出了著名的《秋风辞》。『秋风起兮白云飞，草木黄落兮雁南归』，他和群臣在祭祀后土之际，『泛楼船兮济汾河，横中流兮扬素波』。面对盛大的欢乐，这位踌躇满志的君主却发出了对于时光的喟叹：『欢乐极兮哀情多，少壮几时兮奈老何！』秋风楼因藏有此辞之碑而得名。而秋风楼正是万荣后土祠的压轴建筑。农耕年代，祭祀后土是帝王要务。余晖脉脉，千古胜地诉说着人们对土地的敬畏，这是深植于民族基因中的密码。

万荣 后土祠、秋风楼

摄影 尚建周

## 万荣 汾河入黄处

在万荣庙前村北的高崖下，寂寞而执着的大河迎来了另一条河流的加入。像赴一场约会，汾河从宁武管涔山启程，南行约七百公里，抵达晋南大地，与流经此地的黄河交汇。两大河流冲击之处，地势平坦，河道纵横。播种、耕耘、收获，周而复始，农人们遵循自然之道，勤勉而踏实地安度着每一个日子。

摄影 薛 俊

万荣汾河入黄处

摄影 王修筑

## 宁武 汾河源头

汾河是黄河第二大支流，是山西最大的河流，是三晋儿女的母亲河。临汾、汾阳、襄汾……这些地名足以证明她在山西人民心目中的地位。这里就是汾河的源头，绿树葱茏，水波轻荡，万物清洁而明净。

摄影 贺子毅

宁武 汾河源头

摄影 贺子毅

娄烦 汾河水库

摄影 武涛

娄烦 汾河水库

摄影 尚建周

永济 晋陕黄河特大桥

摄影 尚建周





## 永济 鹳雀楼

唐才子王之涣是否想到，一首视角独特、胸襟开阔、富含哲理的五言绝句，会让蒲州鹳雀楼从此名扬天下？『白日依山尽，黄河入海流』，落日长河的图景被勾勒得淋漓尽致。登楼极目，黄河是那般肃穆壮美，安详从容。遗憾的是，鹳雀楼在元初被毁，但其盛名历久不衰，所幸近年重建，我们的思古之幽情，我们对黄河的心驰神往，终于有了寄托和着落。

## 芮城　风陵渡

风、陵、渡。这三个简单的汉字组合在一起，不知为何，竟让人产生一种心动又茫然的感觉。略带清冷，充满古意，这里会发生多少悱恻迷离的故事呢？风陵渡位于黄河东转拐角处，是晋陕豫三省交通要塞。忆往昔看今朝，焕然一新的古老渡口宠辱不惊，是因为见过尘世太多的波诡云谲和悲欢离合。

摄影 尚建周

大禹像

摄影 尚建周





## 芮城 大禹渡

位于芮城神柏峪的大禹渡，在秦晋豫三省交界处，以治水圣人的名字命名，使其自带不同寻常的光环。从古至今，这里流传着太多与黄河与大禹有关的动人传说。在古代，大禹渡是驿道和盐运之地，商贾不绝，舟楫塞港；在今天，便利的交通让渡口繁华依旧。古渡散发的光芒刺穿时空，光耀此刻，愈显璀璨。

# 芮城 大禹渡黄河湾

摄影 薛俊

坚守安全红线
揭开新篇章

# 运城 运宝高速黄河大桥

# 运城 盐池

在秦晋豫黄河转弯处，晋南盆地的腹地，盐池静静地躺着，人们对其开发利用，已达四千多年。这被誉为『中国死海』的内陆咸水湖，在阳光下，闪烁着红、褐、蓝、紫、金等色彩。那奇异的斑斓之景呈现出阔大而神秘的气象。据传，久远的年代，舜曾轻抚五弦琴吟唱《南风歌》，『南风之薰兮，可以解吾民之愠兮；南风之时兮，可以阜吾民之财兮』。彼时，这位贤德的君王，正将深邃的目光投向那一池雪白坚硬的盐，而南风，正缓缓拂过广袤的河东大地。

摄影 武涛

## 平陆 天鹅湖

黎明时分，静谧的蓝色仿若轻纱笼罩着天地。一群天鹅再次如约而至。这些飞翔高度可达九千米以上的高傲而纯洁的大鸟，从上世纪八十年代起，每年十一月至次年二月，都会从西伯利亚迁徙至平陆的黄河湿地。整个冬天，她们在湖中嬉戏、鸣唱，为湿地增添生机，为人们带来美丽和欢乐。

摄影 武涛

摄影 郑社奎

平陆天鹅湖

馁的精神和认定目标便勇往直前的气魄。黄河不但是中华民族的母亲河，亦系中华文明肇始的源头和起点，更是中华文化的徽号、图腾与旌幡。黄河之水，奔流到海，润我华夏。

# 黄河

YELLOW RIVER

黄河水百折千转，屈曲回圜，跌宕起伏，汹涌澎湃，克服千难万险，一往无前，汇入大海，象征中华民族在历史长河中饱经沧桑而绝不气

黄河水百折千转，屈曲回圜，跌宕起伏，汹涌澎湃，克服千难万险，一往无前，汇入大海，象征中华民族在历史长河中饱经沧桑而绝不气馁的精神和认定目标便勇往直前的气魄。日寇入侵、民族危亡、国难当头时，那首著名的抗日救亡歌曲，便是《黄河大合唱》。

THE COURSE OF TH

SYMBOL OF THE CHINE

AFTER EXPERIENCING TRIB

PUSH STRAIGHT FORWARD

WAS A FAMOUS SONG NA

DURING THE WAR OF

AGGRESSION WHE

E YELLOW RIVER TO THE SEA IS A
SE PEOPLE'S INDOMITABLE SPIRIT
ULATIONS AND THE COURAGE TO
TO THE DESTINATION. AND THERE
MED THE YELLOW RIVER CANTATA
RESISTANCE AGAINST JAPANESE
N THE COUNTRY WAS IN DANGER.

This is Shanxi 这里是山西

图书在版编目（CIP）数据

表里山河 / 贾新田主编 . — 太原：山西教育出版社，2021.5

ISBN 978-7-5703-1465-2

Ⅰ. ①表… Ⅱ. ①贾… Ⅲ. ①名胜古迹—介绍—山西—图集 Ⅳ. ①K928.702.5-64

中国版本图书馆CIP数据核字（2021）第048008号

表里山河

出 版 人：李　飞
责任编辑：刘晓露
复　　审：郭志强
终　　审：杨　文
编辑助理：王兴刚
装帧设计：王春声 郭冰奇
设计助理：闫　荔
装帧监制：赵　群

出版发行：山西出版传媒集团·山西教育出版社
（地址：太原市水西门街馒头巷7号
电话：0351-4729801　邮编：030012）
印　　装：深圳市国际彩印有限公司

开　　本：430mm × 226mm　1/8
印　　张：16.25
字　　数：30千字
版　　次：2021年5月 第1版　2021年5月 深圳第1次印刷
书　　号：ISBN 978-7-5703-1465-2
定　　价：680.00元

# THE GREAT WALL

# 表里山河 长城

MOUNTAINS AND RIVERS OF SHANXI

贾新田 主编

山西出版传媒集团 山西教育出版社

《表里山河》

主　编　贾新田
学术统筹　王修筑
图片统筹　武　涛
内文撰稿　王宝库　白　宁
英文翻译　王介功　崔　璟
设计总监　王春声
篆　刻　唐　晋

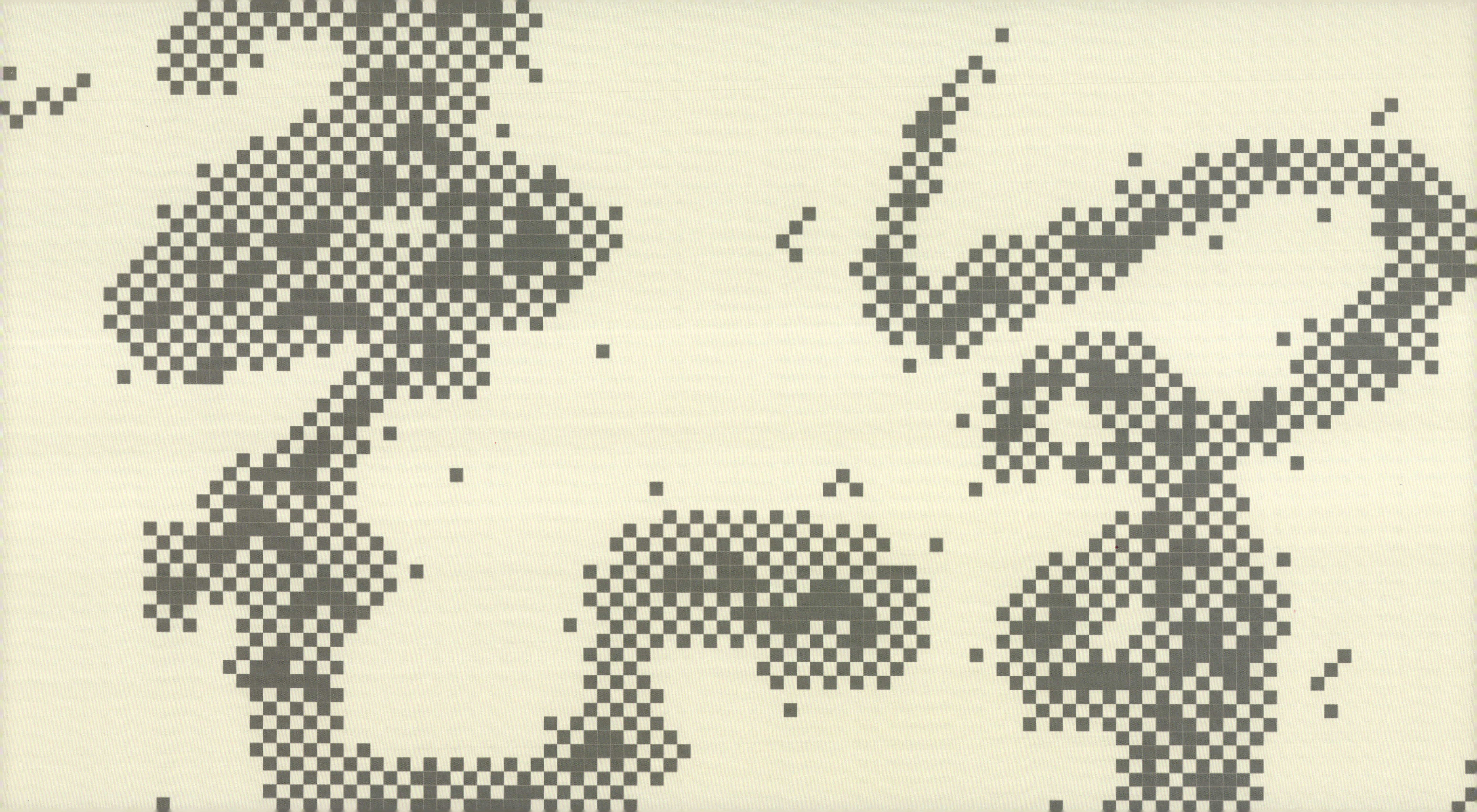

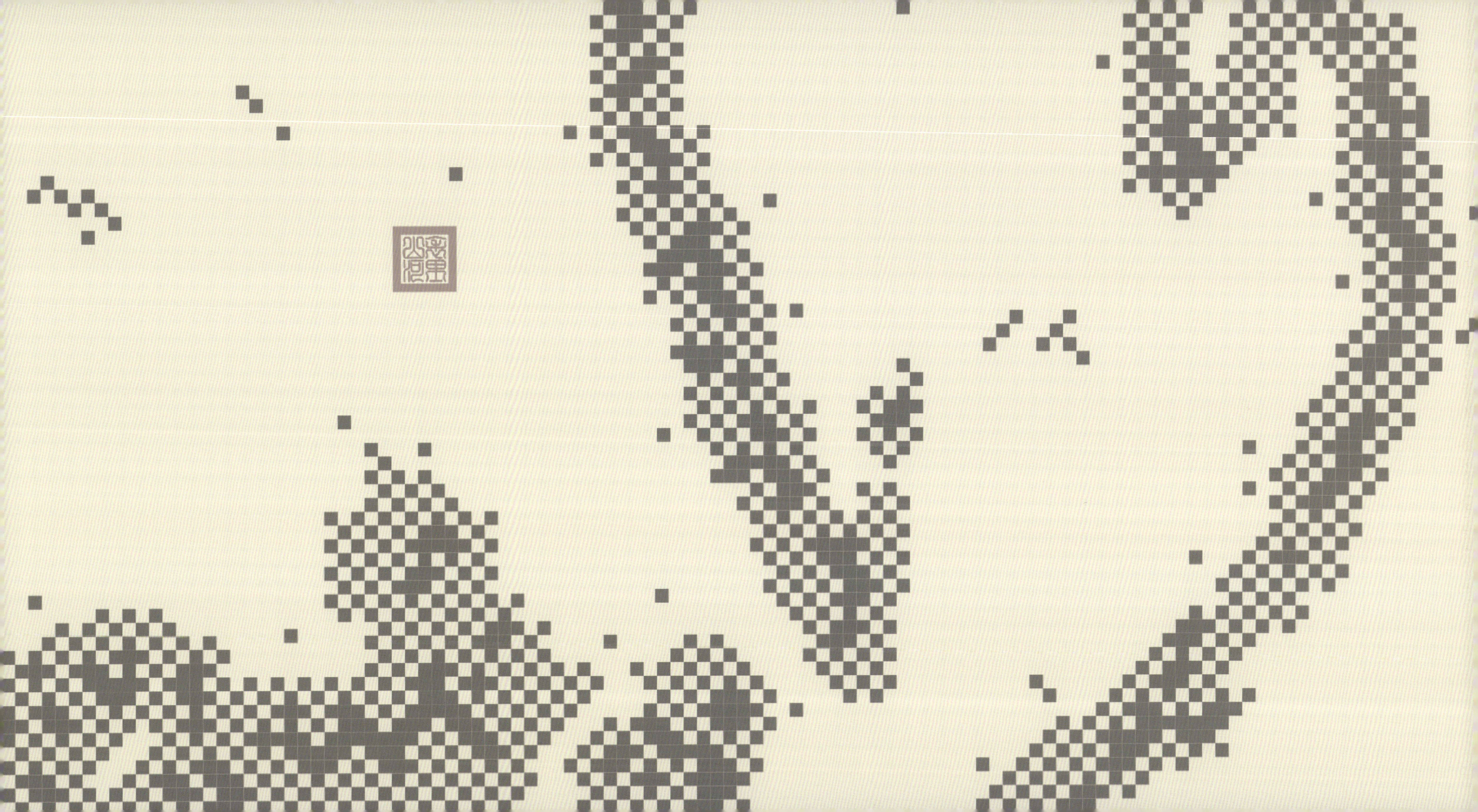

汾澮縈流於右漳沁包絡於左則原隰可以灌注漕粟可以轉輸矣且夫越臨晉泝龍門則涇渭之間可折箠而下也出天井下壺關邯鄲井陘而東不可以惟吾所向乎是故天下之形勢必有取於山西也

山西之形勢最爲完固關中而外吾必首及夫山西蓋語其東則太行爲之屏障其西則大河爲之襟帶於北則大漠陰山爲之外蔽而勾注雁門爲之內險於南則首陽底柱析城王屋諸山濱河而錯峙又南則孟津潼關皆吾門戶也

摄影 任彦龙

大同 长城
Datong Great Wall

On the west of the Taihang Mountains on the second-level platform of the mainland of China, there is a province named "Shanxi" (literally means "on the west of the Mountains"). The origin of its name comes from its location.

Shanxi is the present name, and it was called "Hedong" (literally means "on the east of the River") in ancient times, which was derived from its location on the east of the Yellow River.

The Mountains and the River from which the ancient and modern names of Shanxi originated are extraordinary. The Taihang Mountains are the backbone of the Chinese nation, the pillar of the Chinese territory. The Yellow River is the mother river of the Chinese nation and the emblem, flag and totem of Chinese culture.

The name of Shanxi changes with the change of the capital. In the heyday of the Yellow River civilization, the capital was Chang'an, and the Yellow River was its eastern barrier. Therefore, the province on the east of the Yellow River was named "Hedong". In the booming period of marine civilization, the capital is Beijing, and the Taihang Mountains are its western barrier. So, the province is named "Shanxi" for the similar reason. Being an auxiliary to the ancient and modern capitals of China, Shanxi is very important. Because of this, Shanxi has long history, rich culture and infinite charm.

When we say "knowing Shanxi from the mountains and rivers", we mean to learn the history, culture and charm of Shanxi through the outer and inner parts of Shanxi.

The outer part here refers to the Taihang Mountains, the Yellow River and the Great Wall on the periphery of Shanxi, while the inner part refers to the rivers, mountains and cultural relics of Shanxi. Gu Zuyu, a geographer in the early Qing Dynasty, gave a wonderful statement on this:

Judging from the physical features, Shanxi is closed and complete. I would like to consider Shanxi first beyond the central part of China. To the east, the Taihang Mountains act as a barrier; to the west, the big river is the belt; to the north, the desert and the Yin Mountains are the outer cover, while the Gouzhu Mountain and the Yanmen Pass are the inner barrier; to the south, the Shouyang Mountain, Dizhu Mountain, Xicheng Mountain and Wangwu Mountain scatter along the rivers; to the south of these mountains, Mengjin County and Tong Pass are its gateway. With the Fen River and Hui River on the right, and the Zhang River and Qin River on the left, the fields can be watered and grains transported. And if you go across Linjin Town and continue upstream over Longmen Port, you can easily go down along the Jing River and Wei River. When you go out of the basin here and down Huguan County, along Handan City and Jingxing County to the east, you can reach everywhere. Therefore, considering the physical features of China, Shanxi is the irreplaceable communications center.

This passage outlines the mountains, rivers, passes and ports in Shanxi, and provides a geographical map of ancient Shanxi.

The division of Shanxi's cultural and tourism resources is diverse, but there are always overlaps and omissions. The division based on the three major sectors of the Taihang Mountains, the Yellow River, and the Great Wall is not only scientific and accurate, but also well-documented in history.

It is scientific and accurate. The area of Shanxi is an irregular parallelogram. The Fen River, the mother river of the people of Shanxi, passes through the land from the north to the south. The Taihang Mountains Sector is to the east, and the Yellow River Valley and the Lüliang Mountains are to the west. To the north of the source of Fen River is the so-called the Great Wall Sector.

It is well-documented in history. As Gu Zuyu said, "On the east, the Taihang Mountains act as a barrier." This refers to the Taihang Mountains Sector. "To the west, the big river is the belt" refers to the Yellow River Sector. "To the north, the desert and the Yin Mountains are the outer cover, while the Gouzhu Mountain and the Yanmen Pass are the inner barrier" refers to the Great Wall Sector. As for the central and southern regions, they belong to the Taihang Mountains Sector and the Yellow River Sector with a clear boundary.

In terms of time, the Taihang Mountains, the Yellow River and the Great Wall have long histories, and there are no other comparable geographical things in China. In terms of space, the geographical advantages occupied by these three sectors are even higher. In terms of culture, the richness and uniqueness of the culture here are worth deep exploration. If you sink into it and concentrate on it, you will definitely harvest a lot.

中国大陆第二级台地上的太行山西侧，有一个以“山西”为名号的省份。其名称之缘起，即因位于太行山西侧而得之。

山西是今名，其古称曰“河东”，因位于黄河之东而得之。

山西古今名称缘起的这一山一河，非比寻常。太行山是中华民族的脊骨、中华大厦的栋梁。黄河则是中华民族的母亲河和中华文化的徽号、旗帜与图腾。

山西古今名称之演变，系因国都的改变而改变。黄河文明鼎盛期的最佳国都在长安，黄河乃其东部屏障，斯省所在之地域因而称名“河东”；海洋文明勃兴期的国都定位北京，太行山乃其西部屏障，故斯地名之曰“山西”。山西其地是中国都城的左辅或右弼，因而地理位置得天独厚，十分重要。正因为如此，斯地因而富含了绵远悠长的历史、丰硕厚重的文化和魅力无穷的风韵。

我们说“表里山河看山西”，就是说要透过山西的“表”和“里”看山西的历史、看山西的文化、看山西的风韵。

此处所谓“表”者，是形成山西外围的太行山、黄河与塞外长城，“里”则是山西其地的河流山川与文物风情。清代著名学者顾祖禹对此有十分精彩的表述：

山西之形势，最为完固。关中而外，吾必首及夫山西。盖语其东，则太行为之屏障；其西，则大河为之襟带；于北，则大漠、阴山为之外蔽，而句注、雁门为之内险；于南，则首阳、底柱、析城、王屋诸山，滨河而错峙；又南，则孟津、潼关，皆吾门户也。汾、浍萦流于右，漳、沁包络于左，则原隰可以灌注，漕粟可以转输矣！且夫越临晋，溯龙门，则泾、渭之间，可折箠而下也。出天井，下壶关，邯郸、井陉而东，不可以惟吾所向乎？是故天下之形势，必有取于山西也！

这一段话概括地勾勒出一幅山西全境雄关险隘、襟山带河的水陆形胜图，令人发思古之幽情，平添感慨。

山西文化和旅游资源之板块划分，方法非止一端，但总会产生重叠或遗漏而有失偏颇。作太行、黄河、长城之三大板块划分，既科学精准，又于史有据，可谓是“表里山河看山西”之全息彰显也。

我们说如此划分科学精准，是因为山西地域呈不规则的平行四边形，山西人民的母亲河——汾河由北而南自山西大地穿过，东则太行山板块，西乃黄河流域及其所依傍之吕梁山系。汾源以北的另一方地域，就是所谓长城板块。

我们说如此划分于史有据，即顾祖禹所云“其东，则太行为之屏障”，太行山板块也；“其西，则大河为之襟带”，黄河板块也；“于北，则大漠、阴山为之外蔽，而句注、雁门为之内险”，长城板块也。至于中南部地域则分属太行、黄河两大板块，界限分明，不会重叠。

就时间而言之，太行、黄河、长城的历史之悠久，在大中国的同类地理事物中无有可与攀比者；就空间而言之，此三大板块所占据的地理区位优势更是高踞首位；就文化和韵味而言之，此三大板块文化蕴涵的厚重与丰硕，以及韵味的奇奥与独特，既一言难尽其详，又因观者的不同而各有品味。倘能沉身于其中并且潜心于其内，必定感触良多而收获宏丰。

# THE GREAT WALL 长城

# 长城

THE GREAT WALL

山西是修建长城较多的省份，总长度为1400余千米，包括战国、汉、北魏、北齐、五代、明6个历史时期修筑或使用的长城墙体及附属设施。

# 长城抒怀

LYRICS TO THE GREAT WALL

大中国北部有一道东自山海关起，西到嘉峪关止的蔚为壮观的长墙，号称“长城”。

山西长城之建，可上溯至战国，直至明朝。明朝称长城曰“边墙”，划设九边重镇，山西一省境内居然设置了两个边镇，分别为大同边镇和太原边镇（亦称“山西边镇”）。

建长城是为了防守而非进攻，中国人基因中的和平天性据此可知。古人因险设关，因关建城，因城置镇，因镇开市，关、城、镇、市，战时的军事用途与平时的市井功能兼而有之。

山西境内多长城，自然也就多关隘。斯地关隘设置之巅峰期，当属明代无疑。彼时九边重镇之一的大同边镇所辖之边墙在山西北境，东起天镇之镇口台，西抵偏关鸦角山，全长 647 里，沿线分东西北中四路设防。太原镇边墙西起保德，抵和顺黄榆岭关，全长 1600 余里。

偏头、宁武、雁门概称“三关”，其中偏头关乃大同、太原二边镇扼塞之首，与宣化和大同二边镇呈三角鼎峙之势，而“宣大以蔽京师，偏头以蔽全晋也”。雁门关系代县第一扼要之冲，两侧有十八隘口。宁武关亦有十二堡之险，史称“三关中路之备”。北境之外，山西中南部的关隘更是多得不可胜计。

三晋大地关山重叠，险碍遍布。凭吊这些古关隘，似乎可见可闻狼烟四起、战鼓轰鸣、刀枪闪光、战马嘶叫、朝代更迭……一场场恶战在长城下、关隘前展开，其雄阔威烈，令人闻之魂飞而思之心动。

在长城的接合部、转折处与制高点上，矗立着一座座封闭式的高垒式建筑，是为烽火台。古时每有敌情，这些烽火台昼则青烟缭绕，夜则火光闪耀，自远而近，由此及彼，绵延不断。获得烟火信息的守备部队闻风而动，策马飞驰，列阵对敌，一场场伴随着刀光剑影的厮杀随之展开，于是“烽火”便成为战争的代名词而延用至今。

长城以其工程的浩大和艰辛、历史的古老和凝重、形制的奇特和壮观、气势的飘逸和雄浑，博得了国人的特别钟爱和尊崇，并成为联合国公布的世界文化遗产，享誉全球。

In the north of China, there is a spectacular wall named the Great Wall which extends east to west from Shanhai Pass to Jiayu Pass.

The construction of the Great Wall in Shanxi could date back to the Warring States Period and up to the Ming Dynasty. During the Ming dynasty, the Great Wall was known as the border wall. There were nine frontier counties then, and two were actually set up in Shanxi, which were Datong and Taiyuan (also known as Shanxi Frontier Counties).

The Great Wall was built as protection against various nomadic groups rather than to initiate attack, which demonstrates the peaceful nature of the Chinese people. The ancient Chinese established passes on steep terrains, built walls based on the passes, set up towns behind the walls, and opened up commercial districts in the towns. Passes, walls, towns, and commercial districts, with a combination of military use in wartime and market function in peacetime, played an important role in the life of ancients.

The Great Wall in Shanxi is long, so there are many passes here. The pinnacle of setting up passes in Shanxi was undoubtedly in the Ming Dynasty. The border wall of Datong Frontier County was in the north of Shanxi, starting from Zhenkoutai of Tianzhen County in the east and ending at the Yajiao Mountain in Piantou Pass in the west, with a total length of 647 miles, and was fortified along four lines towards different orientations. The border wall of Taiyuan Frontier County starts from Baode County in the west and reaches Huangyuling Pass in Heshun County, with a total length of about 1600miles.

Piantou, Ningwu and Yanmen are generally known as the Three Passes. Piantou Pass, the most important pass for Datong and Taiyuan, was in a situation of tripartite confrontation with the frontier counties of Xuanhua and Datong. This is just like what ancients said: "Protecting the capital with Xuanhua and Datong; protecting Shanxi with Piantou." Yanmen Pass, which has eighteen other passes on both sides, is the most vital traffic artery of Daixian County. Ningwu Pass has a solid fortification system including twelve fortresses, known as "the Complete Pass in the Middle" in the history. In addition to those on the northern border, there are countless other passes in south-central Shanxi.

On the land of Shanxi, mountains and passes overlap each other while steep terrains and obstacles are everywhere. When you look at these ancient passes with reverence and admiration, you would find as if the rising of beacon-fire, boom of war drums, flashes of blades, roars of warhorses, and change of dynasties are right in front of you. A series of fierce battles that launched under the Great Wall and in front of the passes are so magnificent and imposing that appeal to everyone who has heard of them.

At the junctions, turning points and commanding heights of the Great Wall, there stand many enclosed, high-built constructions known as beacon towers. In ancient times, whenever soldiers became aware of an approaching enemy's army, these beacon towers would filled with smoke by day and fire by night, stretching from far to near, from one to another. The garrison force who received the information from the smoke and fire would move at once, gallop out, form their tactical formation, and start a battle against the enemy. For this reason, the beacon-fire has become synonymous with war and been used ever since.

The Great Wall, with its vast and arduous engineering, its long history, its peculiar and spectacular shape, and its imposing appearance, has been declared a World Cultural Heritage by the United Nations. It has won the special love and respect of the people from China, and also enjoyed a global reputation.

摄影 刘小新

# 长城，中华民族的精神象征

The Great Wall, the spiritual symbol of the Chinese nation

摄影 武涛

天镇长城

摄影 任彦龙

# 天镇 保平堡长城

万里长城从河北怀安进入山西天镇。天镇长城一向以坚固、雄伟著称。保平堡筑于明代，与桦门堡、平远堡、新平堡、瓦窑堡并称『墙外五堡』。嘉靖三十七年，蒙古兵由此入犯。保平堡曾是保障完好的城堡，如今已无人烟。古旧苍凉的景色，空令后人吊古伤今，唏嘘叹惋。

摄影 武涛

天镇 保平堡长城

摄影 武涛

## 天镇 李二口长城

二〇二〇年十一月二十四日，李二口长城段入选第一批国家级长城重要点段名单。远远望去，李二口长城从山脚向山顶爬行的姿势，像一个裸露着身躯的农夫，在命运的摧残中不屈地抗争。那一座座敌楼，是艰难路途中粗重的喘息，也是漫长旅途中短暂的停顿。

## 阳高 守口堡长城

蜿蜒而上，连绵不绝，守口堡长城似在讲述一个一集接一集的连续故事，将人们的思绪拉回到数百年前烽烟四起、战马嘶鸣的年代。王霸雄图，终成过往；古今人事，皆为笑谈。

摄影 王林

## 阳高 长城乡长城

长城乡长城享有盛名，源于其独有的构筑特色，每一座敌楼前方五十米处都建有一个独立的敌楼，外围有一方形窄墙包围，窄墙与长城相连。独立敌楼与长城形成犄角之势。岁月苍茫，戍边将士的身影与长城凝为一体，融入远方的风景。

## 阳高 三墩长城

从来不敢轻率着笔，深恐笔端轻佻，亵渎了历史的神圣与庄严。数百年来，这些残破但骄傲的身躯，无怨无悔肃穆伫立，任凭寒来暑往，不惧雨雪风霜，展示着刚毅而坚韧的性格。

阳高十墩长城

摄影∴王林

摄影 王修筑

大同长城

## 大同 得胜堡

得胜堡建于明万历年间，是大同镇中的重要布防地。得胜堡周围与镇羌堡、四城堡以及边关、得胜口等，组成了一个严密的防御体系。这里，在南北交锋之际烈马嘶鸣；及至和平时期，则是一派贡使不绝、商队接踵的兴盛景象。那份悲壮与繁华，如今都已被雨打风吹去。

摄影 徐劲松

摄影/解学红

摄影/解学红

大同 元墩段长城

摄影 武涛

摄影 张向东

## 右玉 三十二长城

右玉三十二长城从默默无闻到声名鹊起，如梦幻般神奇。人们毕竟还是钟情于能够呈现原初风貌的景物。每一个残破孤独的古堡里，都寄居着古代勇士不死的灵魂；每一道泥土剥落的城墙上，都存留着电闪雷鸣的时光影像。萧萧寒风中，我们似乎仍然能够听到古战场震耳欲聋的呐喊。

杀虎口

## 右玉 杀虎口

右玉杀虎口原名「杀胡口」，清朝政府为避免民族矛盾改「胡」为「虎」。杀虎口是山西省山地与内蒙古草原接壤之处，它是兵家必争之地，又是地位重要的税卡，还是祖祖辈辈山西人背井离乡、艰辛走过的「西口」，至今通道上的老石桥还保存完好。往事如烟，一丝一缕渗入残垣断壁。

摄影 杨东

右玉 杀虎口

## 右玉 铁山堡

右玉号称是『中国古堡之乡』，右玉七十二堡声名远播。铁山堡建于嘉靖三十八年，黄土夯筑，万历年间包砖。铁山堡由两个堡并排而成，呈日字形。一个坚硬的名字，一种奇特的造型，逗引着人们无尽的思古幽情。

摄影 武涛

## 朔州 八岔口

八岔口又称『水芹口』，是雁门十八隘之一，建于明代，与白草口相连接。雁门关古代的防御体系称为『两关四口十八隘』，『两关』为西陉、雁门，『四口』为白草口、广武口、南口和太和岭口。『十八隘』则指水峪、马兰、八岔、元冈等隘口。『两关四口十八隘』，真当得起『雄关漫道，固若金汤』之誉。

## 平鲁长城

平鲁长城为明外长城大同段最西的部分，西北与内蒙古以长城为界，是大同镇的『边墙』。长城沿线，敌楼、墩台、烽火台遥相呼应。黄土不是无情物，它的粗糙，它的坚硬，它的沉默不语，都饱含怜惜与护佑的深情。

摄影 王兴刚

## 平鲁败虎堡

平鲁败虎堡是明代著名的『隆庆议和』发生地。史载，隆庆四年，俺答之孙率人来降，之后明朝借此契机与蒙古达成封王、通贡、互市的协议。北部边防从宣府到嘉峪关的战事基本结束，形成了一段边关无战事的难得的局面。

偏关 柏杨岭长城

摄影 解学红

# 偏关 老牛湾堡

长城与黄河在此不期然地交汇，城与河的握手造就了引人遐想的神奇景观。一路奔腾咆哮的黄河，瞬间变得温顺；而蜿蜒西向的长城，至此与黄河并肩携手。多少年来，望河楼在崖头默默伫立，像一位智者，凝视着川流不息的河水，陷入无边的沉思之中。

沿着晋蒙峡谷黄河岸边修筑的长城也称『黄河边』，这是山西长城中独有的防御建筑。其中桦林堡和寺沟这样的沿河长城，随地形夯筑，与群山和黄河共同构成了浑朴而壮丽的塞外风光。

# 偏关 寺沟长城

摄影 王兴刚

摄影 王兴刚

## 偏关 老营堡

偏关老营堡北控平鲁，西衔偏关，东接宁武，是外长城自柏杨岭向南延伸的内长城上的第一堡，军事位置十分重要。民间有『铜偏关，铁宁武，生铁铸的老营堡』之说。

## 河曲 长城

河曲长城位于晋蒙陕三省交界之地，捍卫山右，屏藩京师，明代处于防御鞑靼、瓦剌的第一线。河曲长城筑于黄河岸边，与黄河相伴而行百余里，有『双龙并行』之美誉。

河曲 长城敌楼

摄影 徐劲松



## 岢岚 长城

岢岚长城采用石块垒砌，沿山过岭，建造艰难，是山西长城中比较特殊的一处遗迹。有人认为岢岚长城是仅存的宋长城，推翻了学术界长期以来认为宋代没有修筑长城的论断，但此说尚需进一步佐证。

摄影 武涛

# 宁武 长城

宁武关北屏大同，南扼太原，西应偏关，东援雁门。北方游牧民族南下掠掳，经常选择宁武关为突破口，故而战争最是频繁。崇祯年间明军与李自成军惨烈一战，更是让宁武关威震天下。岁月无情，却带不走那撼人心魄的故事。

摄影 王修筑

宁武关

摄影 武涛

宁武 阳方口长城

摄影 解学红

## 应县 大石口长城

应县大石口长城是雁门十八隘口之一，当年亦是屯兵重地。时至今日，边墙重镇早已凋零残破，坍塌的烽燧以各种奇怪的姿势兀立在旷野之中，似有郁结之气需要倾吐。

# 山阴 旧广武城

广武旧城位于勾注西陉北口，是农耕民族与游牧民族征战的前沿阵地。宋辽之战，亦在这里反复上演。清风拂过故垒，城池雄风犹在，令游人驻足，令骚客感慨。

摄影 杨东

摄影 王林

# 山阴广武长城

广武素有『北方锁钥』之称。广武长城始于山阴县新广武村，至代县白草口村，是大同一线长城防线被突破后护卫中原的第二道防线，与山下的广武城形成完整的防御群。蓝天白云之下，广武长城雄姿英发，跃舞于绵延群山之上。

广武长城月亮门

摄影 任丽萍

山阴 广武长城

摄影 张向东

代县 雁门关长城

# 代县 雁门关

雁门，多么富有诗意的名字，两山之间，黑色的大雁上下翻飞，有如舞蹈的精灵。然而，雁门却自古就笼罩在征战之中。赵破匈奴，蒙恬击胡，李广神勇，杨业忠烈……一段段令人血脉贲张的历史在这里连续上演。『三关冲要无双地，九塞尊崇第一关』，词雄字健，准确地表现了雁门关『天下九塞，雁门为首』的地位。

摄影 杨东

摄影 杨 东

摄影 杨东

摄影 张向东

代县 白草口猴儿岭

# 繁峙 韩庄长城

繁峙北临雁同，西近雁门，境内长城蜿蜒曲折，享有盛名。韩庄长城是保存较为完好的一段，于此可领略繁峙长城的风貌与神韵。置身于群山环抱之中，行走在长城古道上，自有一股凛然之气自胸中升起。

摄影 徐劲松

# 繁峙 茨沟营长城

二〇二〇年十一月二十四日，明长城茨沟营段入选第一批国家级长城重要点段名单，这是山西长城的骄傲。岁月拂去长城表面的斑驳，呈现于世人眼前的，是古老建筑的沧桑之美。

摄影 李旭光

摄影 杨 东



## 灵丘 平型关

平型关北有恒山如屏高峙，南有五台巍然耸立，两山之间的带状低地是河北平原北部与山西相通的最便捷通道。平型关所在的平型岭是这条带状低地中隆起的部分，形势极为险要。而让平型关名动天下的，并非历朝历代的征战杀伐，而是一九三七年的平型关大捷。古代关隘的现代演绎，为平型关增添了别样的魅力。

摄影 杨东

灵丘 平型关

摄影 张向东

灵丘 荞麦茬长城

天下第九關

# 平定 娘子关

女子的柔弱与长城的刚强，形成了巨大的反差。很难想象，这样险要的关隘，竟然与一位高贵的公主有关。唐朝在此设立戍守处，据传由太宗之姊率女兵驻守，从此肃穆庄严的古长城被涂抹上一丝轻灵、生动的色彩。夜色中的娘子关雾气缭绕，朦胧而神秘，令人不由得怀想与喟叹！

摄影 杨东

## 平定 固关长城

固关长城古为赵长城，已有两千多年的历史，算是长城家族中的最长者了；它还是太行八陉中井陉西出通道。固关曾名『故关』，虽地当冲要，而险不足恃，于是嘉靖二十二年西迁十里筑新城，改『故』为『固』，从此固关名副其实，担负起『京畿藩屏』的要务。固关危楼耸峙，雄奇壮美，有『小八达岭』之称。

摄影：武涛

摄影 杨东

# 平定 固关长城

摄影 解学红

宁武关亦有十二堡之险，史称『三关中路之备』。北境之外，山西中南部的关隘更是多得不可胜计。长城以其工程的浩大和艰辛、历史的古老和凝重、形制的奇特和壮观、气势的飘逸和雄浑，博得了国人的特别钟爱和尊崇，并成为联合国公布的世界文化遗产，享誉全球。

偏头、宁武、雁门概称『三关』，其中偏头关关乃大同、太原二边镇扼塞之首，与宣化和大同二边镇呈三角鼎峙之势，而『宣大以蔽京师，偏头以蔽全晋也』。雁门关系代县第一扼要之冲，两侧有十八隘口。

长城以其工程的浩大和艰辛、历史的古老和凝重、形制的奇特和壮观、气势的飘逸和雄浑，博得了国人的特别钟爱和尊崇，并成为联合国公布的世界文化遗产，享誉全球。

# THE GREAT WALL, WITH ITS V
# ITS LONG HISTORY, ITS PEC
# AND ITS IMPOSING APP
# WORLD CULTURAL HERITAC
# WON THE SPECIAL LOVE AN
# CHINA, AND ALSO

AST AND ARDUOUS ENGINEERING,
ULIAR AND SPECTACULAR SHAPE,
EARANCE, HAS BEEN DECLARED A
E BY THE UNITED NATIONS. IT HAS
RESPECT OF THE PEOPLE FROM
ENJOYED A GLOBAL REPUTATION.

This is Shanxi 这里是山西

**图书在版编目（CIP）数据**

表里山河 / 贾新田主编．— 太原：山西教育出版社，2021.5

ISBN 978-7-5703-1465-2

Ⅰ．①表… Ⅱ．①贾… Ⅲ．①名胜古迹—介绍—山西—图集 Ⅳ．①K928.702.5-64

中国版本图书馆CIP数据核字（2021）第048008号

**表里山河**

**出 版 人**：李　飞
**责任编辑**：刘晓露
**复　　审**：郭志强
**终　　审**：杨　文
**编辑助理**：王兴刚
**装帧设计**：王春声 郭冰奇
**设计助理**：闫　荔
**装帧监制**：赵　群

**出版发行**：山西出版传媒集团・山西教育出版社
（地址：太原市水西门街馒头巷7号
电话：0351-4729801　邮编：030012）
**印　　装**：深圳市国际彩印有限公司

**开　　本**：430mm × 226mm　1/8
**印　　张**：16.25
**字　　数**：30千字
**版　　次**：2021年5月 第1版　2021年5月 深圳第1次印刷
**书　　号**：ISBN 978-7-5703-1465-2
**定　　价**：680.00元

TAI HANG

# 表里山河 太行

MOUNTAINS AND RIVERS OF SHANXI

贾新田 主编

山西出版传媒集团 山西教育出版社

《表里山河》

主　编　贾新田
学术统筹　王修筑
图片统筹　武　涛
内文撰稿　王宝库　邓吉中
英文翻译　王介功　崔　璟
设计总监　王春声
篆　刻　唐　晋

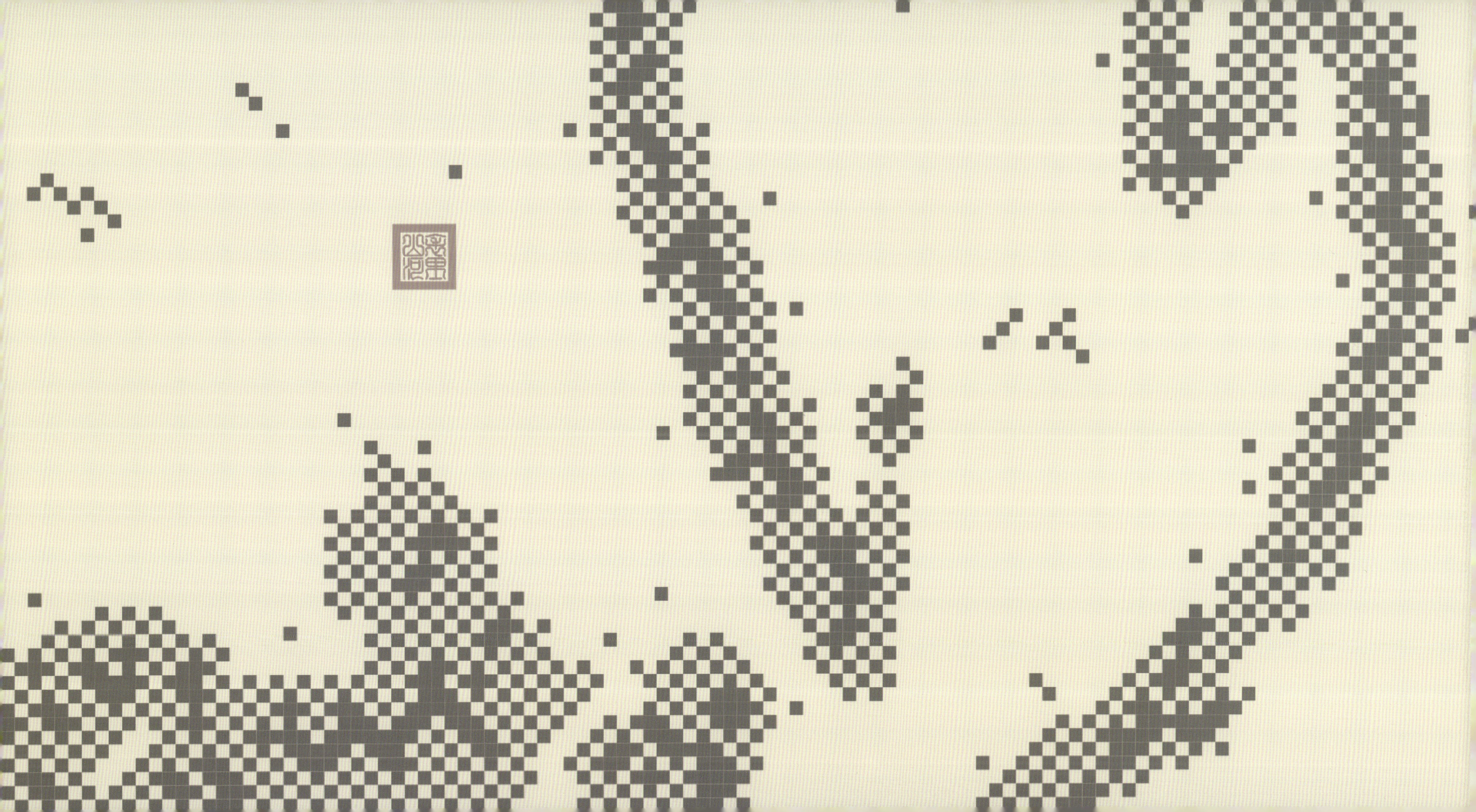

汾澮縈流於右漳沁包絡於左則原隰可以灌注漕粟可以轉輸矣且夫越臨晉泝龍門則涇渭之間可折箠而下也出天井下壺關邯鄲井陘而東不可以惟吾所向乎是故天下之形勢必有取於山西也

山西之形勢最爲完固關中而外吾必首及夫山西蓋語其東則太行爲之屏障其西則大河爲之襟帶於北則大漠陰山爲之外蔽而勾注雁門爲之內險於南則首陽底柱析城王屋諸山濱河而錯峙又南則孟津潼關皆吾門戶也

# 表里山河看山西

KNOWING SHANXI FROM THE MOUNTAINS AND RIVERS

On the west of the Taihang Mountains on the second-level platform of the mainland of China, there is a province named "Shanxi" (literally means "on the west of the Mountains"). The origin of its name comes from its location.

Shanxi is the present name, and it was called "Hedong" (literally means "on the east of the River") in ancient times, which was derived from its location on the east of the Yellow River.

The Mountains and the River from which the ancient and modern names of Shanxi originated are extraordinary. The Taihang Mountains are the backbone of the Chinese nation, the pillar of the Chinese territory. The Yellow River is the mother river of the Chinese nation and the emblem, flag and totem of Chinese culture.

The name of Shanxi changes with the change of the capital. In the heyday of the Yellow River civilization, the capital was Chang'an, and the Yellow River was its eastern barrier. Therefore, the province on the east of the Yellow River was named "Hedong". In the booming period of marine civilization, the capital is Beijing, and the Taihang Mountains are its western barrier. So, the province is named "Shanxi" for the similar reason. Being an auxiliary to the ancient and modern capitals of China, Shanxi is very important. Because of this, Shanxi has long history, rich culture and infinite charm.

When we say "knowing Shanxi from the mountains and rivers", we mean to learn the history, culture and charm of Shanxi through the outer and inner parts of Shanxi.

The outer part here refers to the Taihang Mountains, the Yellow River and the Great Wall on the periphery of Shanxi, while the inner part refers to the rivers, mountains and cultural relics of Shanxi. Gu Zuyu, a geographer in the early Qing Dynasty, gave a wonderful statement on this:

Judging from the physical features, Shanxi is closed and complete. I would like to consider Shanxi first beyond the central part of China. To the east, the Taihang Mountains act as a barrier; to the west, the big river is the belt; to the north, the desert and the Yin Mountains are the outer cover, while the Gouzhu Mountain and the Yanmen Pass are the inner barrier; to the south, the Shouyang Mountain, Dizhu Mountain, Xicheng Mountain and Wangwu Mountain scatter along the rivers; to the south of these mountains, Mengjin County and Tong Pass are its gateway. With the Fen River and Hui River on the right, and the Zhang River and Qin River on the left, the fields can be watered and grains transported. And if you go across Linjin Town and continue upstream over Longmen Port, you can easily go down along the Jing River and Wei River. When you go out of the basin here and down Huguan County, along Handan City and Jingxing County to the east, you can reach everywhere. Therefore, considering the physical features of China, Shanxi is the irreplaceable communications center.

This passage outlines the mountains, rivers, passes and ports in Shanxi, and provides a geographical map of ancient Shanxi.

The division of Shanxi's cultural and tourism resources is diverse, but there are always overlaps and omissions. The division based on the three major sectors of the Taihang Mountains, the Yellow River, and the Great Wall is not only scientific and accurate, but also well-documented in history.

It is scientific and accurate. The area of Shanxi is an irregular parallelogram. The Fen River, the mother river of the people of Shanxi, passes through the land from the north to the south. The Taihang Mountains Sector is to the east, and the Yellow River Valley and the Lüliang Mountains are to the west. To the north of the source of Fen River is the so-called the Great Wall Sector.

It is well-documented in history. As Gu Zuyu said, "On the east, the Taihang Mountains act as a barrier." This refers to the Taihang Mountains Sector. "To the west, the big river is the belt" refers to the Yellow River Sector. "To the north, the desert and the Yin Mountains are the outer cover, while the Gouzhu Mountain and the Yanmen Pass are the inner barrier" refers to the Great Wall Sector. As for the central and southern regions, they belong to the Taihang Mountains Sector and the Yellow River Sector with a clear boundary.

In terms of time, the Taihang Mountains, the Yellow River and the Great Wall have long histories, and there are no other comparable geographical things in China. In terms of space, the geographical advantages occupied by these three sectors are even higher. In terms of culture, the richness and uniqueness of the culture here are worth deep exploration. If you sink into it and concentrate on it, you will definitely harvest a lot.

中国大陆第二级台地上的太行山西侧，有一个以“山西”为名号的省份。其名称之缘起，即因位于太行山西侧而得之。

山西是今名，其古称曰“河东”，因位于黄河之东而得之。

山西古今名称缘起的这一山一河，非比寻常。太行山是中华民族的脊骨、中华大厦的栋梁。黄河则是中华民族的母亲河和中华文化的徽号、旗帜与图腾。

山西古今名称之演变，系因国都的改变而改变。黄河文明鼎盛期的最佳国都在长安，黄河乃其东部屏障，斯省所在之地域因而称名“河东”；海洋文明勃兴期的国都定位北京，太行山乃其西部屏障，故斯地名之曰“山西”。山西其地是中国都城的左辅或右弼，因而地理位置得天独厚，十分重要。正因为如此，斯地因而富含了绵远悠长的历史、丰硕厚重的文化和魅力无穷的风韵。

我们说“表里山河看山西”，就是说要透过山西的“表”和“里”看山西的历史、看山西的文化、看山西的风韵。

此处所谓“表”者，是形成山西外围的太行山、黄河与塞外长城，“里”则是山西其地的河流山川与文物风情。清代著名学者顾祖禹对此有十分精彩的表述：

山西之形势，最为完固。关中而外，吾必首及夫山西。盖语其东，则太行为之屏障；其西，则大河为之襟带；于北，则大漠、阴山为之外蔽，而勾注、雁门为之内险；于南，则首阳、底柱、析城、王屋诸山，滨河而错峙；又南，则孟津、潼关，皆吾门户也。汾、浍萦流于右，漳、沁包络于左，则原隰可以灌注，漕粟可以转输矣！且夫越临晋，溯龙门，则泾、渭之间，可折箠而下也。出天井，下壶关，邯郸、井陉而东，不可以惟吾所向乎？是故天下之形势，必有取于山西也！

这一段话概括地勾勒出一幅山西全境雄关险隘、襟山带河的水陆形胜图，令人发思古之幽情，平添感慨。

山西文化和旅游资源之板块划分，方法非止一端，但总会产生重叠或遗漏而有失偏颇。作太行、黄河、长城之三大板块划分，既科学精准，又于史有据，可谓是“表里山河看山西”之全息彰显也。

我们说如此划分科学精准，是因为山西地域呈不规则的平行四边形，山西人民的母亲河——汾河由北而南自山西大地穿过，东则太行山板块，西乃黄河流域及其所依傍之吕梁山系。汾源以北的另一方地域，就是所谓长城板块。

我们说如此划分于史有据，即顾祖禹所云“其东，则太行为之屏障”，太行山板块也；“其西，则大河为之襟带”，黄河板块也；“于北，则大漠、阴山为之外蔽，而勾注、雁门为之内险”，长城板块也。至于中南部地域则分属太行、黄河两大板块，界限分明，不会重叠。

就时间而言之，太行、黄河、长城的历史之悠久，在大中国的同类地理事物中无有可与攀比者；就空间而言之，此三大板块所占据的地理区位优势更是高踞首位；就文化和韵味而言之，此三大板块文化蕴涵的厚重与丰硕，以及韵味的奇奥与独特，既一言难尽其详，又因观者的不同而各有品味。倘能沉身于其中并且潜心于其内，必定感触良多而收获宏丰。

TAIHANG 太行

# 太行

TAIHANG

太行山在汾河之东，碣石以西，北邻长城，
南界黄河，纵跨山西全境。

# 太行颂歌

ODE TO THE TAIHANG MOUNTAINS

The Taihang Mountains may be called the backbone of the Chinese nation. In ancient times, warlords sprang up everywhere in China to vie for the throne. And the Taihang Mountains were their key battlefields. In modern times, the Eighth Route Army led by the Communist Party stationed in the Taihang Mountains to fight against Japanese aggression, and finally found the PRC.

Lying to the east of the Fenhe River and to the west of the Jieshi Mountain, with the Great Wall in the north and the Yellow River in the south, the towering Taihang Mountains span the entire Shanxi from north to south. According to legend, Yan Di the ancestor of Chinese nation climbed the Yangtou Mountain of the Taihang Mountains to taste all kinds of plants and found crops and herbs for the people. He started the farming civilization of China. And after that, Jingwei the drowned daughter of Yan Di tried to fill up the sea with pebbles, Houyi the greatest archer shot down nine of the ten suns, Nüwa who created humans patched the holes in the sky with stone blocks, and Yugong a foolish old man removed the mountains... We could say that many prehistoric myths of the Chinese nation originated from the Taihang Mountains.

The Taihang Mountains are also known as Daxing (The Big), Wuxing (Five Elements), Wangmu (Queen Mother), Huangmu (Empress Mother) and Nüwa. The terrain of it is gentle to the west and steep to the east. There are eight passes from south to north, which were called the Eight Passes of Taihang in ancient times. The first is Zhiguan Pass; the second is Taihang Pass, the third is Bai Pass; the fourth is Fukou Pass, the fifth is Jing Pass; the sixth is Feihu Pass, the seventh is Puyin Pass; the eighth is Jundu Pass. Being the backbone of China, the Taihang Mountains of course have more than just one perilous pass.

In the south of the Taihang Mountains, there are beautiful Mang River, Mount Wangmang and the Grand Canyon of Taihang. And in the north, there are perilous Pingxing Pass and the famous Buddhist site of Mount Wutai. What a combination of majesty, danger and beauty! They are like paintings and poems that draw admiration of the visitors.

On the tops of the Taihang Mountains, you could see the long winding roads, peaks and ridges, towering rocks, deep valleys, forests, waterfalls, stone niches, huts hidden in the bushes, blooming flowers, cooking smoke, village girls washing clothes in streams, and old men playing Chinese chess.

In the morning, you could enjoy the magnificent sunrise on the top. Looking down the cliff, you could see broad farmlands and crisscrossing roads.

太行山堪称中华民族之脊骨。古时天下大乱群雄并起，太行山乃问鼎天下之枢纽；近代倭寇入侵民族危亡，八路军据太行逐鹿中原，终乱世而兴新邦。

太行山在汾河之东，碣石以西，北邻长城，南界黄河，纵跨山西全境。其势高耸而与天为党，其气雄浑令地脉坤康。相传，炎帝登上党太行羊头山尝百谷而得嘉禾、尝百草而获良药，开创了农耕文明，令华夏光耀地球东方。唯如是，故炎帝之女精卫填海、帝尧猛士后羿射日、人祖女娲炼石补天、北山愚公矢志移山……诸多中华民族之史前期神话，缘此而发端于太行。

太行又以“大形”“五行”“王母”“皇母”“女娲”诸名为山之名号。上党大地雄踞太行最高处，地势西缓东陡，自南而北布列通道八条，古称“太行八陉”，其一曰“轵关陉”，其二曰“太行陉”，其三曰“白陉”，其四曰“滏口陉”，其五曰“井陉”，其六曰“飞狐陉”，其七曰“蒲阴陉”，其八曰“军都陉”。夫太行为天下脊，岂止一方之险要而已！

太行南有蟒河、王莽岭之秀及其大峡谷之奇，北有平型关之险以及佛教圣地五台山之胜，融雄奇、险秀、阳刚、浑厚于一体，雄浑壮阔，似画如诗，已臻大雄至美、出神入化之境界，瞻之愈胜，仰之弥高。

登临太行绝巅，但见山势萦回旋绕，渐次高升，山径弯弯曲曲，绵远悠长，峰峦叠嶂，危岩高耸，沟深林密，瀑流垂练，石龛半嵌于崖腰，茅屋隐现在树丛，繁花似锦，炊烟如缕，村姑浣衣，老翁对弈。朝阳如火球喷吐烈焰，自云海山峦间蓬勃跃出，偶尔有彤霞弥漫，光芒万丈，景象瑰丽而壮观。自悬崖边探身俯视，但见田畴沃野，阡陌纵横。

拾级而上，但见百转千回中，却有古刹梵宫镶嵌于危峰，坐落在峭壁，钟鼓之声可闻，正是“阶穷道尽疑无路，门启洞开又一层”。山上之木结构古建筑成了历史年轮，懿耶美哉！爰撰歌颂之曰：

Climbing up the steps, you could see ancient Buddhist temples on peaks and cliffs, and hear the sounds of bells and drums. Every time you think there is a dead end in front, you will find a new road around the corner. Such ancient buildings and splendid scenery urge me to praise them with a poem:

The towering Taihang Mountains are as high as the sky.
Like heaven, they give the idea of strength in the motion;
Like the earth, they have the capacity and sustaining power.
The farming civilization also started here in the Yangtou Mountain.
How majestic and splendid they are,
Like an ethereal fairyland, or a gallery of poetry and painting.
They are the pillar of the country, which lasts forever.

巍巍太行，与天为党。
天行乾健，地势坤康。
始肇农耕，羊头山上。
雄浑壮阔，大气阳刚。
空灵仙境，诗画长廊。
国脉悠长，国家栋梁。

摄影 秦国增

# 太行，中华民族的脊梁

Taihang, the backbone of the Chinese nation

摄影 马明标

## 灵丘　灵丘故道

位于大同市灵丘县，是北魏时期开凿的由山西高原北部通往华北平原的交通要道。它见证过鲜卑民族的崛起，聆听过战马嘶鸣的声音，守护过问鼎天下的梦想。而今英雄已逝，千年的历史只留下了斑驳的印迹，遥远的车轮和脚步声仿佛仍然回响。

灵丘故道上的觉山寺塔

摄影：任丽萍

位于阳泉市盂县梁家寨乡的深山沟谷中，是盂县保存最完整的古村落。坐落在一处巨石山坡上，依山就势而建，自下而上共有十多层，屋瓦相连，参差错落，相依相偎。老村、老树、老屋、老街、老人……这里的一砖一瓦、一阶一木、一楼一碾，都弥漫着惹人沉醉的气息。

## 盂县 大汖村

天下第一

## 盂县 藏山

位于阳泉市盂县苌池镇藏山村东，相传为赵氏孤儿故事的发生地。北倚五台山，南望娘子关，危岩若削，掩映古刹之香火；涧水潺湲，平添楼台之谐趣。古刹殿堂皆依山傍壁而筑，同自然景观珠联璧合，相映成趣。

摄影：武涛 高智

## 盂县 十八盘

位于阳泉市盂县北下庄乡，地处白马山中段，自古就是通往河北平山的重要隘口。人说沟壑是太行山的皱纹，千万年的阻隔是历史的无奈。如今十八道曲折盘旋的通途，在时光的流水中穿梭，有云雾装点，有红叶陪伴，饱经沧桑的太行刹那间焕发青春的容颜。

摄影 张向东

## 昔阳 鹤度岭

位于晋中市昔阳县与河北省交界的山梁上，古称『仙人台』。传说中唯有仙鹤能飞度的极峰，留下了先民的足迹，那是在峭壁之间筑起的一道关隘。千百年来，那雄鹰振翅的模样，一直在静静诠释着『一夫当关，万夫莫开』的坚定信念。

位于晋中市和顺县东部的太行山断裂带，与河北省接壤。山高沟深，石巨水险，放眼所及可达两省三县。晨观云海日出，飘渺变化无穷；晚看千峰夕照，苍山层林尽染。此处兼太行风光、栈道天险、南方山林、北国草原特色于一体，令人神往。

## 和顺 走马岭

摄影 任丽萍

位于晋中市左权县的太行山断层边缘，与河北接壤。山西一侧地势相对平缓，河北一侧则骤然下降，石崖相连，绝壁成排。极目瞩望，千山万壑之间，林莽岩穴之上，水气蒸腾，浓雾翻滚，犹如千万条神龙吞吐气息，变幻无穷，神秘莫测。

## 左权 太行山

摄影 武涛

摄影 张向东



# 左权 太行山

左权 麻田

摄影：张向东

## 武乡 板山

位于长治市武乡县洪水镇，是通往黎城黄崖洞的咽喉要冲，人称其为八百里太行的观景台。历史的沧桑不能消磨那青春的容颜，千峰竞秀的雄姿扑面而来。那满山堆锦的红叶，那变幻无常的云海，那霞光缭绕的日出，仿佛上天馈赠的瑰丽画卷。

武乡 板山

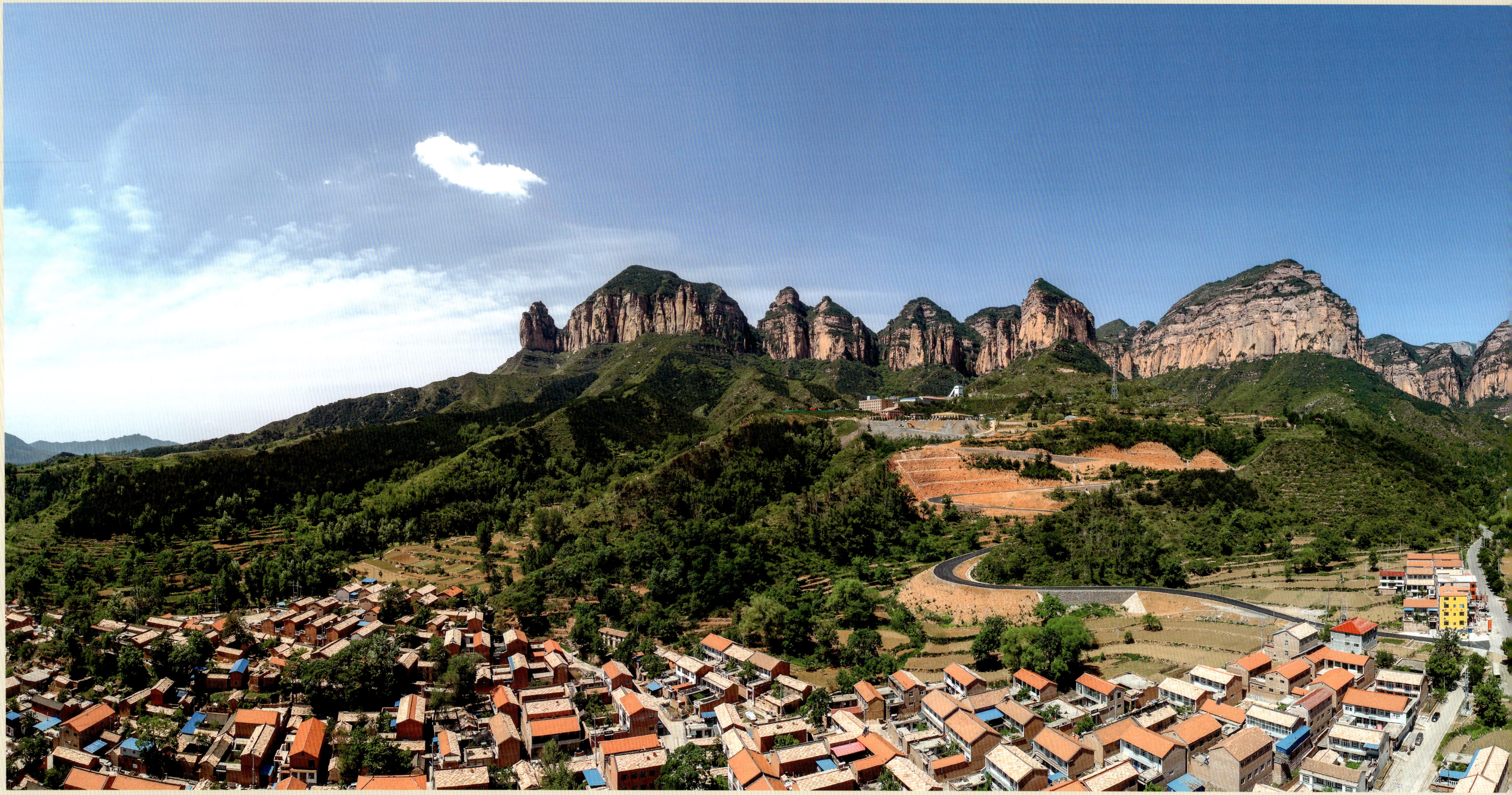

## 黎城 太行山

位于长治市黎城县，集山、水、泉、瀑为一体。箭岭削岩，望之屏气息声；碧岫丹崖，临之心旷神怡。又有黄栌在秋，霜染红叶；白松驻冬，迎风傲雪。石洞、小峡、古寺、天梯，置身其境，直叹雄奇之景无绝，而天人之感不尽也。

摄影：王修筑

黄崖洞

摄影：武涛

摄影 陆小玲

黎城 板山

摄影 任吉刚

摄影 杨 军

∴ 摄影 徐劲松

## 长治 太行梯田

位于长治市。那不是层层梯田，那是太行山飘逸妩媚的衣褶，刻画着春天播种的脚印，缠绕着秋天收获的希望。每一道梯田都承载着一个美丽的中国梦，每一处山凹都隐藏着一座岁月静好的太行人家。虽没有小桥流水，却也会有古道西风。若能寄身于此，夫复何求？

## 山野人家

袅袅炊烟，小小村落，这里不止是太行山一隅，更是我念兹在兹的故乡。秋天来了，漫山遍野的黄栌、红枫、银杏奔放了各自的颜色，搭配幽静恬淡的青砖碧瓦，这便是与世无争的太行人家，这便是游子心中的精神家园。

摄影 武涛

## 平顺 井底村

位于长治市平顺县东寺头乡，好似小小的婴孩，在太行山健硕的怀抱缱绻幽眠。刀削斧劈的悬崖，一线通幽的峡谷，千奇百怪的山石，甘甜可口的山泉，碧波荡漾的深潭，引人入胜的溶洞，多处古老的庙宇遗址……杵臼、磨碾，鸡犬之声相闻，山村野趣，令人神往。

摄影 王修筑

平顺 岳家寨

摄影 王修筑

平顺 虹霓村

天脊山

## 平顺 天脊山

位于长治市平顺县境内。『上党从来天下脊』，道出此名之神韵。荟萃太行山水之精华，奇、险、绝、秀、幽，缺一不可；绝壁、深峡、飞瀑、清潭、奇栈，让人叹为观止。那百米坐佛，兼得自然和人工之妙，栩栩如生，不知望尽了多少过眼烟云，看破了多少世间百态！

摄影 王兴刚

摄影 王修筑

平顺 太行天路

摄影 武涛

平顺 太行山大峡谷

## 平顺 太行山通天峡

位于长治市平顺县境内，横跨晋、豫两省，与著名的红旗渠相连。其间高峡平湖，既有北方山水的雄浑壮阔，又有江南风光的飘逸妩媚。巨大的石屏山伫立峡间，山体如刀削斧刻般光滑陡峻，就像一座天然屏风，把整个山谷的风景隐藏在身后，邀你去发现。

摄影 王林

摄影 武涛

## 壶关 太行山红豆峡

位于长治市壶关县太行山大峡谷，因境内天然生长珍稀树种红豆杉而得名。两头出口狭窄，腹地开阔，形似葫芦。缘峡而进，两侧直壁断崖绵延矗立，崖间泉眼点点，河谷流水淙淙，飞瀑深潭随处可见。乔灌相间，花果竞艳，藤萝缠绕，盘根错节，诚为峡谷奇观。

## 壶关 太行山八泉峡

位于长治市壶关县太行山大峡谷，因北口崖壁有八个泉眼而得名。峡谷两侧群峰竞秀，万壑争奇。泉源百余处，处处叮咚源远流长；飞瀑几十条，条条咆哮一泻千里。举首仰望，长峡犹如一幅雄奇壮丽的山水长卷，将云山雾水、深峡幽谷、飞瀑激流、奇峰异石集于一身。

壶关 太行山八泉峡

壶关 太行山八泉峡

摄影 王林



## 陵川 王莽岭

位于晋城市陵川县境内。多少个美誉指向这里，『清凉胜境』『避暑天堂』『世外桃源』『太行至尊』，都是实至名归。高低错落的五十多个山峰，云涛涌起，绝壁峥嵘。千沟万壑草木苍翠，珍禽异兽上下齐鸣，丹崖赤壁连绵无绝——这里是仙境般的存在。请敞开心扉，让时光的流云进入。我们都是小小过客，举目瞩望，亿万年前的鸿影仿佛在眼前闪过。

摄影 王林

陵川 王莽岭

太行群山秀

陵川 王莽岭

摄影 刘和平



陵川 王莽岭

摄影 李卫东

陵川 锡崖沟

# 陵川 锡崖沟

位于晋城市陵川县东端，是一道呈南北走向的大峡谷。一定是造物主用巨斧劈成，地壳生生地垂直裂开。峡谷两侧峭壁如屏，砂岩似朱，谷底林木葱郁。一股清泉从壁间飞流而下，涛声如雷，寒气上逼，蔚为壮观。

摄影：王林

摄影 武涛

陵川 锡崖沟挂壁公路

陵川 昆山挂壁公路

# 陵川 白陉古道

这是晋城市陵川县至河南辉县一段保存最完好的古道，全程百余千米。千年的岁月磨蚀了古道的容颜，古道如今已人迹罕至，任凭繁华落尽，只愿在荒僻的深谷守候孤独。那一道道深深的车辙，那一个个弯弯的马蹄印，在无言地诉说着昔日繁华。

摄影 武涛

陵川 白陉古道

摄影 武涛

# 泽州 碗子城

位于晋城市泽州县晋庙铺镇，坐落在太行陉著名的『羊肠坂道』上，扼守晋城、沁阳之要冲。古往今来，它曾接待过多少宿将名帅小憩，曾见证过多少争斗厮杀！夕阳西下，如今的小城依然固若金汤，只是早已不见了昔日的兵来将挡，人喊马嘶。

晋城 丹河大桥

# 忻州 五台山

广义的太行山系包括五台山。五台山位于忻州市境内，因五座高峰山顶如垒土之台而得名，是中国青庙黄庙共处的佛教道场，为四大佛教圣地之首，东汉时佛教即传入此地。塔院寺的大白塔，塔身如藻瓶，气势恢宏，为五台山的标志。梵音缭绕，转身凝望，世间有多少苦难，这千年名山就有多少慈悲。

摄影/李旭光

摄影 徐劲松

忻州五台山

摄影 武涛

忻州 五台山

莫测的沟壑峡谷。

人类在太行山生生不息，诞生出多少有趣的传说和感人的事迹。愚公移山，让太行山深深地刻印在中华民族的传统记忆里；百团大战，让太行山自豪地书写进中国革命的英雄史诗中。

太行山，守候和期盼，演绎和记录，张扬和宣示——中华民族辉煌灿烂的文明篇章。

# 太行

TAIHANG

巍巍太行山，雄浑八百里。亿万年的轮回，伴随着大地的演化，造就了太行山接天拔地、伟岸雄奇的气魄。它荟萃了大自然的鬼斧神工，托举出千姿百态的峰岭崖嶂，刻蚀出变化巍巍太行，与天为党。天行乾健，地势坤康。
始肇农耕，羊头山上。雄浑壮阔，大气阳刚。
空灵仙境，诗画长廊。国脉悠长，国家栋梁。

THE TOWERING TAIH
AS THE SKY.LIKE HE

LIKE THE EARTH, T

THE FARMING CIVILIZ

HOW MAJES

ANG MOUNTAINS ARE AS HIGH
AVEN, THEY GIVE THE IDEA OF
STRENGTH IN THE MOTION;
HEY HAVE THE CAPACITY AND
SUSTAINING POWER.
ATION ALSO STARTED HERE IN
THE YANGTOU MOUNTAIN.
TIC AND SPLENDID THEY ARE.

This is Shanxi 这里是山西

图书在版编目（CIP）数据

表里山河 / 贾新田主编．— 太原：山西教育出版社，2021.5

ISBN 978-7-5703-1465-2

Ⅰ．①表… Ⅱ．①贾… Ⅲ．①名胜古迹—介绍—山西—图集 Ⅳ．①K928.702.5-64

中国版本图书馆CIP数据核字（2021）第048008号

表里山河

出 版 人：李　飞
责任编辑：刘晓露
复　　审：郭志强
终　　审：杨　文
编辑助理：王兴刚
装帧设计：王春声 郭冰奇
设计助理：闫　荔
装帧监制：赵　群

出版发行：山西出版传媒集团·山西教育出版社
（地址：太原市水西门街馒头巷7号
电话：0351-4729801　邮编：030012）
印　　装：深圳市国际彩印有限公司

开　　本：430mm × 226mm　1/8
印　　张：16.25
字　　数：30千字
版　　次：2021年5月 第1版　2021年5月 深圳第1次印刷
书　　号：ISBN 978-7-5703-1465-2
定　　价：680.00元